NOT
Nominated

MOVIE POSTERS

370 GREAT FILMS THAT WERE NOT NOMINATED FOR THE BEST PICTURE ACADEMY AWARD®

volume fifteen of
the illustrated history of movies through posters

Images from the Hershenson-Allen Archive

Previous Volumes:

Edited by Richard Allen and Bruce Hershenson
Published by Bruce Hershenson
P.O. Box 874, West Plains, MO 65775
Phone: (417) 256-9616 Fax: (417) 257-6948
mail@brucehershenson.com (e-mail)
http://www.brucehershenson.com or
http://www.emovieposter.com (website)

SOLD OUT

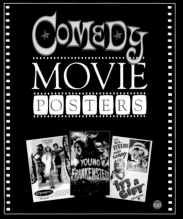

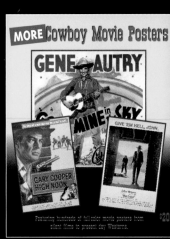

SOLD OUT

INTRODUCTION

Welcome to the fifteenth volume of the Illustrated History of Movies Through Posters. This book is intended to serve as a companion volume to the eighth book of this series, Best Pictures' Movie Posters, which included posters from every film that was nominated for the Best Picture Academy Award®. This volume has posters from five worthy films from every year the Academy Award® has been presented that were NOT nominated for the Academy's top award, as well as hundreds of equally worthy "honorable mentions", that could only be listed by name because of space limitations.

It is intended to alert the reader to great films they may have never seen, for all too often attention is focused on the nominated films, and many fine "also-rans" are forgotten. An excellent case could be made that many of these films are equal to, or superior to those that were nominated, but I leave the readers to make their own determinations as to the relative merits of the films. Because I also include all the names of the winners and the nominated films, this volume serves as an easy reference to the greatest films ever made, letting you quickly see what year a film was made, whether or not it won or was nominated for the Best Picture Academy Award®, and whether or not it is currently available on video (see below).

I urge everyone reading these words to make the effort to eventually view all of the films listed within these pages. Altogether there are 1150 films, and I think you will find all of them well worth watching! Over 90% of the films are available for purchase on VHS (those that are currently unavailable are marked with an asterisk after the title). **You can have them in your hands in a matter of days by ordering them from Movies Unlimited, the greatest source of video's and DVDs! Call them at 800-4-MOVIES (800-466-8437) or visit their website at** http://www.moviesunlimited.com (The 10% that are unavailable from them are sure to eventually be re-issued, and some may be found through websites such as eBay that sell out-of-print videos).

How were these films selected? First, I compiled all the "Greatest Films" that I could find, resulting in a massive list of several thousands of films. The only ground rule I set was to NOT consider any films not made in English ("foreign films") or documentaries, for these films, while not specifically excluded from the Best Picture award, were virtually never nominated, and I wished this volume to focus more on films that the Academy members HAD considered, but had rejected for reasons of their own. Besides, I plan to devote future volumes of this series to non-English language films and to documentaries, so I will defer consideration of them until that time. I did ignore the unusual idiosyncrasies of how the Academy selected films (in the first few years, films were chosen on a split year basis, and in some years up to twelve films were nominated). There are also odd rules about determining in which year a film is eligible for consideration. I chose to ignore all this and to simply chose five films from every year from 1927 to 2000, using the commonly accepted year of release.

I organized a jury of eight movie poster collectors (my partner Richard Allen, Nelson Black, Joe Burtis, Marty Davis, Mike Hawks, Mike Kaplin, David Kusumoto, John Skillin and myself) who I knew to be lifelong film buffs and gave each of them my preliminary list, having each "vote" for up to five films per year, but with the stipulation that they had to have personally seen every film they voted for (no voting based on reputation!). I also included the votes of Bob King (editor of Classic Images), my wife, brother, and uncle (Sylvia Hershenson, Mark Hershenson, and Eli Post), and also those of my oldest employee, Phillip Wages. I know that each found this a most enjoyable chore, but I wish to give them my heartfelt thanks. I compiled all the votes and the consensus determined which films made the "final cut" for this volume. Certainly one might argue with which films were and were not selected, and I invite you to do so! Please e-mail or write me with a list of any films you felt should have been included, or ones you would have excluded, and the day this first edition of this book sells out I will begin work on a second edition that incorporates the most voted-on reader suggestions.

I next needed to locate images from all the selected films. I already had over 90% of the images in the archive I co-own with my partner, Richard Allen, the Hershenson-Allen Archive. The archive consists of over 35,000 different movie poster images, all photographed directly from the original posters onto high quality 4" x 5" color transparencies. There is not another resource like it anywhere, and it is the world's foremost source of movie poster images. The Archive has provided images for books, video's, DVDs, magazines, and newspapers. To find the remaining images I needed I turned to two collectors who have helped me many times in the past. One is Mike Hawks, the world's foremost collector of lobby cards, who provided me with title or scene lobby cards from many of the most difficult early films. The other is Ira Resnick, who owns the MPA Gallery in New York City, one of the oldest and largest movie poster galleries. Between his personal collection and the MPA Gallery inventory, Ira was able to provide most of the remaining titles I needed. Finally, I was down to a short list of titles and three generous longtime collectors, Marty Davis, Jon Schwartz and Jim Sendek, and two major dealers, Rotman Collectibles and MovieGoods.com, provided those last titles. All of these folks went a great deal out of their way to help me find these rare titles, and I give them my deepest thanks.

Unless otherwise noted, the image in this volume is of the original U.S. one-sheet poster (the standard movie poster size, measuring 27" x 41"), from the first release of the film. Other sizes included are lobby cards (11" x 14"), window cards (14" x 22"), inserts (14" x 36"), half-sheets (22" x 28"), three-sheets (41" x 81"), six-sheets (81" x 81"), and foreign posters (varying sizes). **This is not a catalog of posters for sale, nor do I sell any sort of movie poster reproductions!** However, I do sell movie posters of all sorts through public auctions, both "live" and over the Internet. If you are interested in acquiring original vintage movie posters (or any of the other books I have published) visit my website at http://www.brucehershenson.com (the most visited vintage movie poster site on the Internet) or send me a self-addressed stamped envelope for free brochures.

More so than any of my previous books, this book required a huge amount of date-checking and proofreading, to ensure that all the dates are accurate. I need to thank Angie Fish, Libby Lowe, and Sylvia Hershenson, who assisted in its preparation and did the date-checking and proofreading. I also need to thank Amy Knight who did the layouts and designed the covers for this book. Most of all, I need to thank my partner, Richard Allen. He has always loved movie posters of all years and genres, and he tracked down many of the images in this book. We share a common vision, and we hope to keep publishing these volumes until we have covered every possible genre of film.

I dedicate this book to the memory of one of the very first and greatest collectors and dealers of movie posters and lobby cards, Bob Colman. Many collectors made their first purchases of posters from Bob, and he was liked by everyone who came in contact with him. I miss him very much and I know that sentiment is shared by many many others in the hobby.

Bruce Hershenson
April 2001

1927: What **WAS** Nominated for the Best Picture Academy Award®: **Wings**, Seventh Heaven*.

Here are five worthy films made in 1927 (in no particular order) that the Academy did ***NOT*** nominate for Best Picture:

1. THE GENERAL, half-sheet

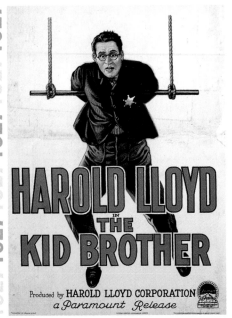

2. SUNRISE*, lobby card

3. UNDERWORLD

4. THE KID BROTHER*, window card

5. THE BELOVED ROGUE, title lobby card

Honorable Mentions (other worthy films that also were **NOT** nominated for Best Picture): College, It, The Jazz Singer, The Unknown*.

Note: The film that WON the Best Picture Academy Award® is in ***BOLD*** type. Films that are not presently available for purchase on VHS cassette have an asterisk (*) after their title.

Here are five worthy films made in 1928 (in no particular order) that the Academy did **NOT** nominate for Best Picture:

6. THE WIND

7. STEAMBOAT BILL, JR., title lobby card

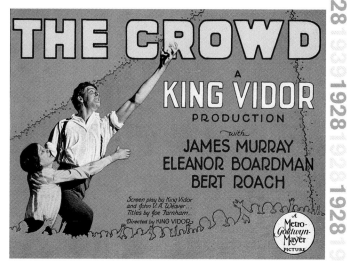

8. THE CROWD, title lobby card

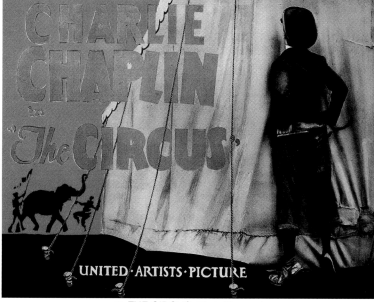

9. THE CIRCUS, title lobby card

10. THE WEDDING MARCH

Honorable Mentions (other worthy films that also were **NOT** nominated for Best Picture):
Beggars of Life*, The Cameraman, The Docks of New York, The Last Command, Show People

Note: The film that WON the Best Picture Academy Award® is in **BOLD** type. Films that are not presently available for purchase on VHS cassette have an asterisk (*) after their title.

1928

1929: What **WAS** Nominated for the Best Picture Academy Award®:

The Broadway Melody, The Hollywood Revue*, In Old Arizona*, Alibi, Disraeli, The Love Parade*

Here are five worthy films made in 1929 (in no particular order) that the Academy did **NOT** nominate for Best Picture:

11. THE VIRGINIAN*

12. HALLELUJAH, title lobby card

13. BULLDOG DRUMMOND, three-sheet

14. THE COCOANUTS, insert

15. BLACKMAIL, Australian daybill

Honorable Mentions (other worthy films that also were **NOT** nominated for Best Picture): Condemned*, The Divine Lady*, Queen Kelly, Spite Marriage, The Wild Party*

Note: The film that WON the Best Picture Academy Award® is in **BOLD** type. Films that are not presently available for purchase on VHS cassette have an asterisk (*) after their title.

1930: What **WAS** Nominated for the Best Picture Academy Award®: **All Quiet on the Western Front**, The Big House, The Divorcee
Here are five worthy films made in 1930 (in no particular order) that the Academy did **NOT** nominate for Best Picture:

16. MOROCCO

17. MONTE CARLO*, lobby card

18. HELL'S ANGELS, lobby card

19. THE BLUE ANGEL, title lobby card

20. LITTLE CAESAR, window card

Honorable Mentions (other worthy films that also were **NOT** nominated for Best Picture): Animal Crackers, Anna Christie, Applause, Raffles*, With Byrd at the South Pole

Note: The film that WON the Best Picture Academy Award® is in **BOLD** type. Films that are not presently available for purchase on VHS cassette have an asterisk (*) after their title.

1931: What **WAS** Nominated for the Best Picture Academy Award®:

Cimarron, The Front Page, Skippy*, East Lynne*, Trader Horn, Bad Girl*, The Champ, The Smiling Lieutenant*, Arrowsmith, Five Star Final*

Here are five worthy films made in 1931 (in no particular order) that the Academy did **NOT** nominate for Best Picture:

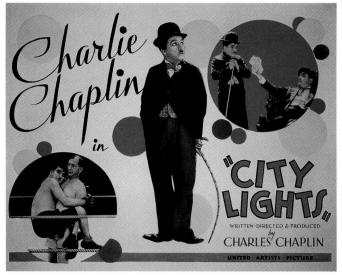

22. CITY LIGHTS, title lobby card

23. DR. JEKYLL AND MR. HYDE, lobby card

21. THE PUBLIC ENEMY, insert

24. FRANKENSTEIN, window card

25. DRACULA, lobby card

Honorable Mentions (other worthy films that also were **NOT** nominated for Best Picture): Monkey Business, Platinum Blonde, Svengali, Tabu

Note: The film that WON the Best Picture Academy Award® is in **BOLD** type. Films that are not presently available for purchase on VHS cassette have an asterisk (*) after their title.

1932: What **WAS** Nominated for the Best Picture Academy Award®:
Grand Hotel, One Hour with You*, Shanghai Express, A Farewell to Arms, Smilin' Through, I am a Fugitive from a Chain Gang

Here are five worthy films made in 1932 (in no particular order) that the Academy did **NOT** nominate for Best Picture:

26. HORSE FEATHERS, 1938 reissue

27. TROUBLE IN PARADISE*, lobby card

28. LOVE ME TONIGHT*, lobby card

29. RED DUST, lobby card

30. SCARFACE, 1937 reissue

Honorable Mentions (other worthy films that also were **NOT** nominated for Best Picture):
Blonde Venus, Jewel Robbery*, Million Dollar Legs, One Way Passage*, Tarzan the Ape Man

Note: The film that WON the Best Picture Academy Award® is in **BOLD** type. Films that are not presently available for purchase on VHS cassette have an asterisk (*) after their title.

1933: What **WAS** Nominated for the Best Picture Academy Award®:

Cavalcade, Lady For A Day, Little Women, 42nd Street, She Done Him Wrong, State Fair*, The Private Life of Henry VIII

Here are five worthy films made in 1933 (in no particular order) that the Academy did **NOT** nominate for Best Picture:

31. COUNSELLOR AT LAW*, lobby card

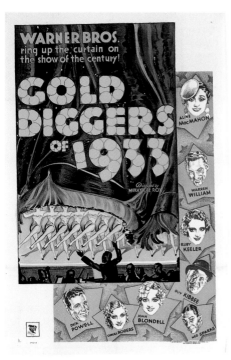

32. GOLD DIGGERS OF 1933

33. KING KONG, three-sheet

34. FOOTLIGHT PARADE, door panel

35. QUEEN CHRISTINA, three-sheet

Honorable Mentions (other worthy films that also were **NOT** nominated for Best Picture):

Duck Soup, Flying Down to Rio, The Invisible Man, Morning Glory*, Sons of the Desert, Topaze*

Note: The film that WON the Best Picture Academy Award® is in **BOLD** type. Films that are not presently available for purchase on VHS cassette have an asterisk (*) after their title.

1934: What **WAS** Nominated for the Best Picture Academy Award®:

It Happened One Night, The Gay Divorcee, The White Parade*, Cleopatra, Here Comes the Navy*, Flirtation Walk, Viva Villa!, The Thin Man, Imitation of Life, One Night of Love*, The Barretts of Wimpole Street, The House of Rothschild*

Here are five worthy films made in 1934 (in no particular order) that the Academy did **NOT** nominate for Best Picture:

37. THE SCARLET EMPRESS, half-sheet

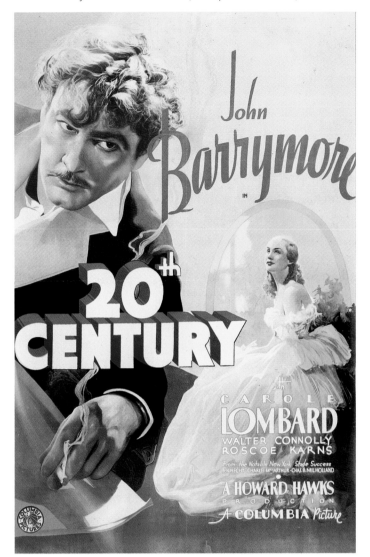

36. 20TH CENTURY

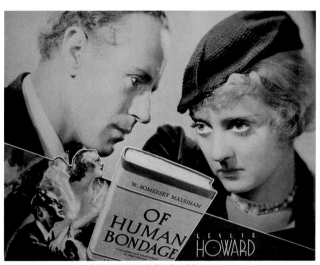

38. OF HUMAN BONDAGE, lobby card

39. IT'S A GIFT, lobby card

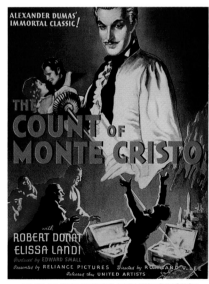

40. THE COUNT OF MONTE CRISTO*, window card

Honorable Mentions (other worthy films that also were **NOT** nominated for Best Picture):
The Black Cat, Death Takes a Holiday, Our Daily Bread, Tarzan and His Mate

Note: The film that WON the Best Picture Academy Award® is in **BOLD** type. Films that are not presently available for purchase on VHS cassette have an asterisk (*) after their title.

1935: What **WAS** Nominated for the Best Picture Academy Award®:

Mutiny on the Bounty, A Midsummer Night's Dream, Alice Adams, Les Miserables, The Lives of a Bengal Lancer, Naughty Marietta, Ruggles of Red Gap, Broadway Melody of 1936*, David Copperfield, The Informer, Captain Blood, Top Hat

Here are five worthy films made in 1935 (in no particular order) that the Academy did **NOT** nominate for Best Picture:

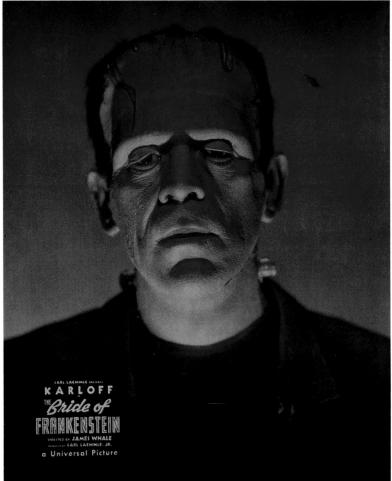

41. BRIDE OF FRANKENSTEIN, jumbo lobby card

42. THE 39 STEPS

43. A NIGHT AT THE OPERA

44. THE GOOD FAIRY*, six-sheet

45. MAN ON THE FLYING TRAPEZE*

Honorable Mentions (other worthy films that also were **NOT** nominated for Best Picture):

Barbary Coast, Sanders of the River, The Scarlet Pimpernel, The Scoundrel*, She

Note: The film that WON the Best Picture Academy Award® is in **BOLD** type. Films that are not presently available for purchase on VHS cassette have an asterisk (*) after their title.

1936: What **WAS** Nominated for the Best Picture Academy Award®: **The Great Ziegfeld**, Anthony Adverse, The Story of Louis Pasteur, A Tale of Two Cities, San Francisco, Romeo and Juliet, Three Smart Girls, Mr. Deeds Goes to Town, Libeled Lady, Dodsworth

Here are five worthy films made in 1936 (in no particular order) that the Academy did **NOT** nominate for Best Picture:

46. SWING TIME, window card

47. MY MAN GODFREY, lobby card

48. FURY, lobby card

49. MODERN TIMES, lobby card

50. SHOW BOAT, window card

Honorable Mentions (other worthy films that also were **NOT** nominated for Best Picture):

The Charge of the Light Brigade, The General Died at Dawn, Lloyds of London, The Petrified Forest, The Plainsman, Things to Come

Note: The film that WON the Best Picture Academy Award® is in **BOLD** type. Films that are not presently available for purchase on VHS cassette have an asterisk (*) after their title.

1937: What **WAS** Nominated for the Best Picture Academy Award®: **The Life of Emile Zola**, The Awful Truth, Dead End, The Good Earth, Captains Courageous, A Star is Born, Stage Door*, In Old Chicago, One Hundred Men and a Girl, Lost Horizon

Here are five worthy films made in 1937 (in no particular order) that the Academy did **NOT** nominate for Best Picture:

51. SHALL WE DANCE, lobby card

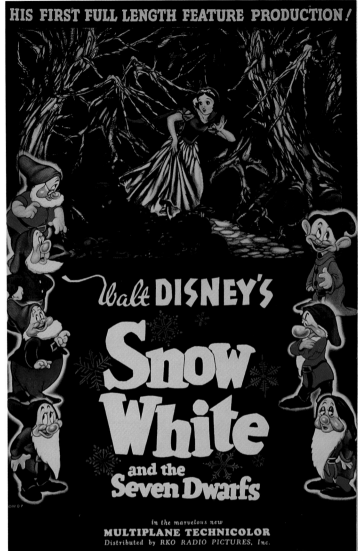

53. SNOW WHITE AND THE SEVEN DWARFS

52. THE PRISONER OF ZENDA, title lobby card

54. A DAY AT THE RACES

55. NOTHING SACRED, lobby card

Honorable Mentions (other worthy films that also were **NOT** nominated for Best Picture): Camille, Fire Over England, Topper*, Way Out West, Wee Willie Winkie

Note: The film that WON the Best Picture Academy Award® is in **BOLD** type. Films that are not presently available for purchase on VHS cassette have an asterisk (*) after their title.

1938: What **WAS** Nominated for the Best Picture Academy Award®: **You Can't Take It with You**, Jezebel, The Citadel, Test Pilot, Boys Town, Pygmalion, Four Daughters, Alexander's Ragtime Band, Grand Illusion, The Adventures of Robin Hood

Here are five worthy films made in 1938 (in no particular order) that the Academy did **NOT** nominate for Best Picture:

56. ANGELS WITH DIRTY FACES

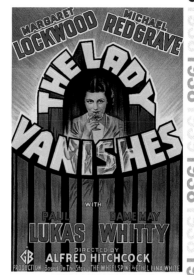

57. THE LADY VANISHES

58. SUEZ*

59. BRINGING UP BABY, lobby card

60. HOLIDAY

Honorable Mentions (other worthy films that also were **NOT** nominated for Best Picture):
Bluebeard's Eighth Wife, The Dawn Patrol, If I Were King, Marie Antoinette, Room Service

Note: The film that WON the Best Picture Academy Award® is in **BOLD** type. Films that are not presently available for purchase on VHS cassette have an asterisk (*) after their title.

1939: What **WAS** Nominated for the Best Picture Academy Award®: **Gone With The Wind**, Stagecoach, Love Affair, Of Mice and Men, Wuthering Heights, Ninotchka, Goodbye, Mr. Chips, Dark Victory, Mr. Smith Goes to Washington, The Wizard of Oz

Here are five worthy films made in 1939 (in no particular order) that the Academy did **NOT** nominate for Best Picture:

61. THE ROARING TWENTIES, three-sheet

62. GUNGA DIN*, three-sheet

63. THE HUNCHBACK OF NOTRE DAME, three-sheet

64. ONLY ANGELS HAVE WINGS

65. DESTRY RIDES AGAIN, lobby card

Honorable Mentions (other worthy films that also were **NOT** nominated for Best Picture):
Babes in Arms, Beau Geste, They Made Me a Criminal, The Women, You Can't Cheat an Honest Man

Note: The film that WON the Best Picture Academy Award® is in **BOLD** type. Films that are not presently available for purchase on VHS cassette have an asterisk (*) after their title.

What WAS Nominated for the Best Picture Academy Award®: **Rebecca**, The Grapes of Wrath, The Long Voyage Home, Kitty Foyle, Our Town, Foreign Correspondent, The Great Dictator, The Philadelphia Story, All This, and Heaven Too, The Letter

Here are five worthy films made in 1940 (in no particular order) that the Academy did *NOT* nominate for Best Picture:

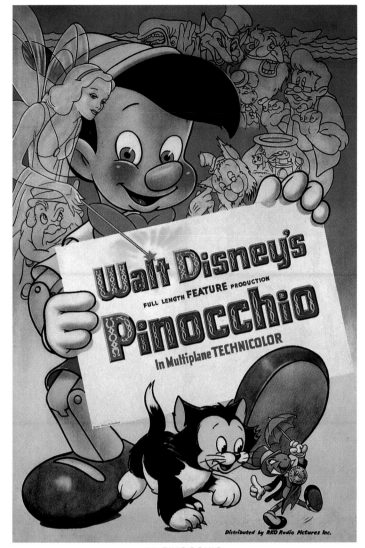

66. PINOCCHIO

67. THE THIEF OF BAGDAD, title lobby card

68. FANTASIA, half-sheet

69. HIS GIRL FRIDAY, lobby card

70. THE SHOP AROUND THE CORNER

Honorable Mentions (other worthy films that also were **NOT** nominated for Best Picture):
The Bank Dick, The Great McGinty, Knute Rockne, All-American, The Mark of Zorro, Northwest Passage, The Westerner

Note: The film that WON the Best Picture Academy Award® is in **BOLD** type. Films that are not presently available for purchase on VHS cassette have an asterisk (*) after their title.

1941: What **WAS** Nominated for the Best Picture Academy Award®: **How Green was My Valley**, Citizen Kane, Blossoms in the Dust, Sergeant York, Hold Back the Dawn*, Here Comes Mr. Jordan, Suspicion, The Little Foxes, The Maltese Falcon, One Foot in Heaven*

Here are five worthy films made in 1941 (in no particular order) that the Academy did **NOT** nominate for Best Picture:

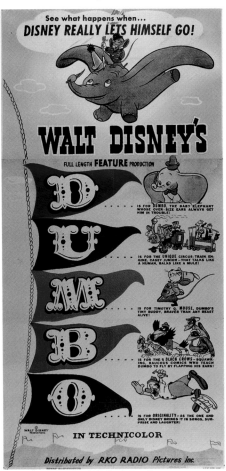

71. DUMBO, three-sheet

72. BALL OF FIRE, three-sheet

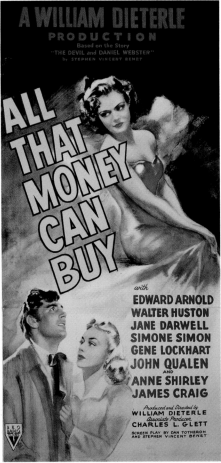

73. ALL THAT MONEY CAN BUY, three-sheet

74. HIGH SIERRA

75. THE LADY EVE, lobby card

Honorable Mentions (other worthy films that also were **NOT** nominated for Best Picture):
The Devil and Miss Jones, Dr. Jekyll and Mr. Hyde, The Strawberry Blonde, You'll Never Get Rich

Note: The film that WON the Best Picture Academy Award® is in **BOLD** type. Films that are not presently available for purchase on VHS cassette have an asterisk (*) after their title.

1942: What **WAS** Nominated for the Best Picture Academy Award®: **Mrs. Miniver**, The Magnificent Ambersons, The Talk of the Town, Kings Row, The Invaders, The Pied Piper*, Random Harvest, The Pride of the Yankees*, Wake Island, Yankee Doodle Dandy

Here are five worthy films made in 1942 (in no particular order) that the Academy did **NOT** nominate for Best Picture:

76. SULLIVAN'S TRAVELS

77. NOW, VOYAGER, lobby card

78. CAT PEOPLE*, lobby card

79. WOMAN OF THE YEAR, title lobby card

80. THE PALM BEACH STORY

Honorable Mentions (other worthy films that also were **NOT** nominated for Best Picture):
Bambi*, Holiday Inn, One of Our Aircraft is Missing, This Gun for Hire, To Be or Not to Be

Note: The film that WON the Best Picture Academy Award® is in **BOLD** type. Films that are not presently available for purchase on VHS cassette have an asterisk (*) after their title.

1943: What **WAS** Nominated for the Best Picture Academy Award®: **Casablanca**, In Which We Serve, The Ox-Bow Incident, For Whom the Bell Tolls, The Human Comedy, Watch on the Rhine, Madame Curie, Heaven Can Wait, The More the Merrier, The Song of Bernadette

Here are five worthy films made in 1943 (in no particular order) that the Academy did **NOT** nominate for Best Picture:

81. SHADOW OF A DOUBT

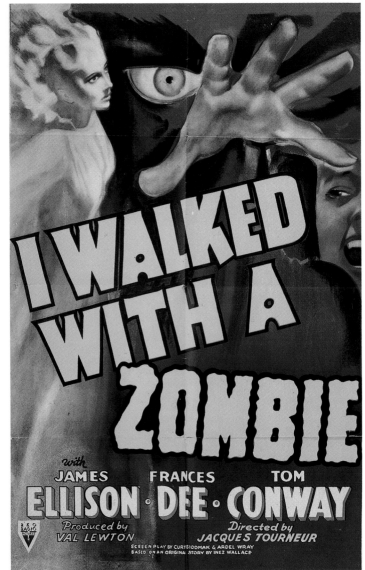

83. I WALKED WITH A ZOMBIE*

82. FIVE GRAVES TO CAIRO

84. THE LIFE AND DEATH OF COLONEL BLIMP*

85. MR. LUCKY*, title lobby card

Honorable Mentions (other worthy films that also were **NOT** nominated for Best Picture):
Cabin in the Sky, Hello Frisco, Hello, Lassie Come Home, Sahara, So Proudly We Hail!

Note: The film that WON the Best Picture Academy Award® is in **BOLD** type. Films that are not presently available for purchase on VHS cassette have an asterisk (*) after their title.

Here are five worthy films made in 1944 (in no particular order) that the Academy did **NOT** nominate for Best Picture:

86. LAURA, three-sheet

87. MEET ME IN ST. LOUIS, insert

88. TO HAVE AND HAVE NOT, three-sheet

89. THE MIRACLE OF MORGAN'S CREEK, lobby card

90. MURDER, MY SWEET

Honorable Mentions (other worthy films that also were **NOT** nominated for Best Picture):
Arsenic and Old Lace, Hail the Conquering Hero, National Velvet, The Woman in the Window

Note: The film that WON the Best Picture Academy Award® is in **BOLD** type. Films that are not presently available for purchase on VHS cassette have an asterisk (*) after their title.

1945: What **WAS** Nominated for the Best Picture Academy Award®:
The Lost Weekend, The Bells of St. Mary's, Mildred Pierce, Spellbound, Anchors Aweigh

Here are five worthy films made in 1945 (in no particular order) that the Academy did **NOT** nominate for Best Picture:

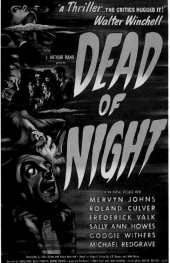

91. DEAD OF NIGHT*

92. LEAVE HER TO HEAVEN

93. SCARLET STREET, six-sheet

94. THEY WERE EXPENDABLE

95. I KNOW WHERE I'M GOING!*, lobby card

Honorable Mentions (other worthy films that also were **NOT** nominated for Best Picture):
And Then There Were None, Blithe Spirit*, The Clock, The Story of G.I. Joe, A Tree Grows In Brooklyn

Note: The film that WON the Best Picture Academy Award® is in **BOLD** type. Films that are not presently available for purchase on VHS cassette have an asterisk (*) after their title.

1946: What **WAS** Nominated for the Best Picture Academy Award®:
The Best Years of Our Lives, Henry V*, It's a Wonderful Life, The Razor's Edge, The Yearling

Here are five worthy films made in 1946 (in no particular order) that the Academy did **NOT** nominate for Best Picture:

96. NOTORIOUS!, insert

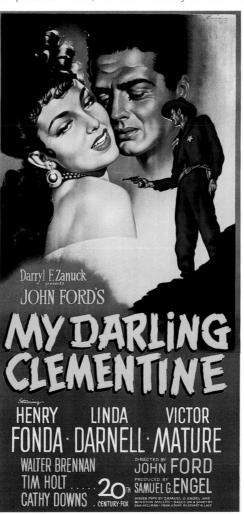

97. MY DARLING CLEMENTINE, three-sheet

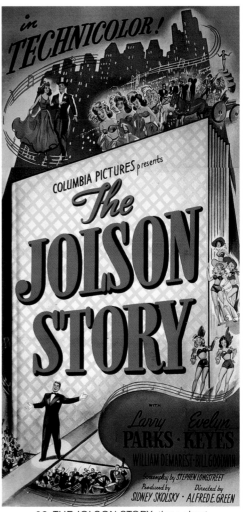

98. THE JOLSON STORY, three-sheet

99. BRIEF ENCOUNTER*, title lobby card

100. THE BIG SLEEP

Honorable Mentions (other worthy films that also were **NOT** nominated for Best Picture):
Duel in the Sun, Gilda, The Killers, A Matter of Life and Death, The Postman Always Rings Twice, The Stranger

Note: The film that WON the Best Picture Academy Award® is in **BOLD** type. Films that are not presently available for purchase on VHS cassette have an asterisk (*) after their title.

1947: What **WAS** Nominated for the Best Picture Academy Award®:

Gentleman's Agreement, Miracle on 34th Street, Crossfire, Great Expectations*, The Bishop's Wife

Here are five worthy films made in 1947 (in no particular order) that the Academy did **NOT** nominate for Best Picture:

101. NIGHTMARE ALLEY*

103. OUT OF THE PAST, 1953 reissue

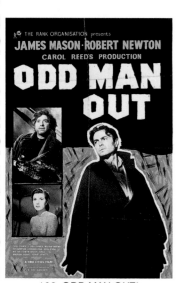

102. ODD MAN OUT*,
English one-sheet

104. THE GHOST AND MRS. MUIR

105. MONSIEUR VERDOUX, title lobby card

Honorable Mentions (other worthy films that also were **NOT** nominated for Best Picture):

Black Narcissus, Body and Soul, Brute Force, Kiss of Death, Life With Father

Note: The film that WON the Best Picture Academy Award® is in **BOLD** type. Films that are not presently available for purchase on VHS cassette have an asterisk (*) after their title.

1948: What **WAS** Nominated for the Best Picture Academy Award®:
Hamlet, The Treasure of the Sierra Madre, The Snake Pit, Johnny Belinda, The Red Shoes*

Here are five worthy films made in 1948 (in no particular order) that the Academy did **NOT** nominate for Best Picture:

106. OLIVER TWIST, lobby card

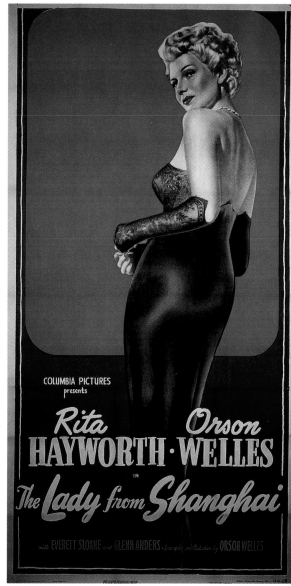

108. THE LADY FROM SHANGHAI

107. MR. BLANDINGS BUILDS HIS DREAM HOUSE, lobby card

109. RED RIVER, lobby card

110. THE WINSLOW BOY

Honorable Mentions (other worthy films that also were **NOT** nominated for Best Picture):
The Big Clock, The Fallen Idol, Force of Evil, Fort Apache, Key Largo, Sorry, Wrong Number

Note: The film that WON the Best Picture Academy Award® is in **BOLD** type. Films that are not presently available for purchase on VHS cassette have an asterisk (*) after their title.

1949: What **WAS** Nominated for the Best Picture Academy Award®:
All the King's Men, Twelve O'Clock High, A Letter to Three Wives, The Heiress, Battleground

Here are five worthy films made in 1949 (in no particular order) that the Academy did **NOT** nominate for Best Picture:

111. SHE WORE A YELLOW
RIBBON

112. WHITE HEAT

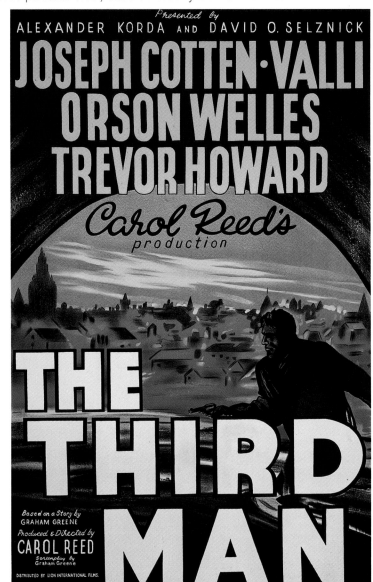

113. THE THIRD MAN, English one-sheet

114. KIND HEARTS AND CORONETS*,
Belgian poster

115. ADAM'S RIB, title lobby card

Honorable Mentions (other worthy films that also were **NOT** nominated for Best Picture): Champion, Criss Cross, On the Town, The Set-Up*, They Live By Night*

Note: The film that WON the Best Picture Academy Award® is in **_BOLD_** type. Films that are not presently available for purchase on VHS cassette have an asterisk (*) after their title.

Here are five worthy films made in 1950 (in no particular order) that the Academy did **NOT** nominate for Best Picture:

116. IN A LONELY PLACE

117. HARVEY, French poster

118. RIO GRANDE, French poster

119. THE ASPHALT JUNGLE, half-sheet

120. THE GUNFIGHTER

Honorable Mentions (other worthy films that also were **NOT** nominated for Best Picture): Cinderella*, D.O.A., Gun Crazy*, Night and the City*, Winchester '73

Note: The film that WON the Best Picture Academy Award® is in **BOLD** type. Films that are not presently available for purchase on VHS cassette have an asterisk (*) after their title.

1951: What **WAS** Nominated for the Best Picture Academy Award®:
An American in Paris, Decision Before Dawn*, A Streetcar Named Desire, Quo Vadis?, A Place in the Sun

Here are five worthy films made in 1951 (in no particular order) that the Academy did **NOT** nominate for Best Picture:

121. THE BIG CARNIVAL*, insert

122. STRANGERS ON A TRAIN, three-sheet

123. THE DAY THE EARTH STOOD STILL, standee

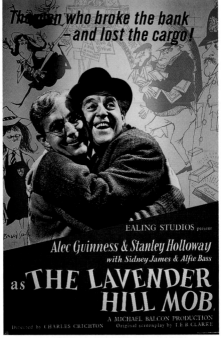

124. THE LAVENDER HILL MOB*,
English poster

125. THE AFRICAN QUEEN*, lobby card

Honorable Mentions (other worthy films that also were **NOT** nominated for Best Picture):
A Christmas Carol, Detective Story*, The Man in the White Suit*, The Thing, When Worlds Collide

Note: The film that WON the Best Picture Academy Award® is in **BOLD** type. Films that are not presently available for purchase on VHS cassette have an asterisk (*) after their title.

Here are five worthy films made in 1952 (in no particular order) that the Academy did **NOT** nominate for Best Picture:

126. SINGIN' IN THE RAIN

127. THE BAD AND THE BEAUTIFUL, title lobby card

128. PAT AND MIKE, title lobby card

129. LIMELIGHT, title lobby card

130. VIVA ZAPATA, Italian poster

Honorable Mentions (other worthy films that also were **NOT** nominated for Best Picture):
The Big Sky*, Come Back, Little Sheba, The Importance of Being Earnest, The Narrow Margin*

Note: The film that WON the Best Picture Academy Award® is in **BOLD** type. Films that are not presently available for purchase on VHS cassette have an asterisk (*) after their title.

1953: What **WAS** Nominated for the Best Picture Academy Award®: **From Here to Eternity**, Roman Holiday, Shane, The Robe, Julius Caesar

Here are five worthy films made in 1953 (in no particular order) that the Academy did **NOT** nominate for Best Picture:

131. THE BIG HEAT

133. GENTLEMEN PREFER BLONDES

132. THE BAND WAGON,
three-sheet

134. PICKUP ON SOUTH STREET

135. STALAG 17, lobby card

Honorable Mentions (other worthy films that also were **NOT** nominated for Best Picture):
Genevieve*, The Naked Spur, Titanic, The War of the Worlds

Note: The film that WON the Best Picture Academy Award® is in **_BOLD_** type. Films that are not presently available for purchase on VHS cassette have an asterisk (*) after their title.

1954: What **WAS** Nominated for the Best Picture Academy Award®:
On the Waterfront, The Caine Mutiny, Three Coins in the Fountain, Seven Brides for Seven Brothers, The Country Girl
Here are five worthy films made in 1954 (in no particular order) that the Academy did **NOT** nominate for Best Picture:

136. JOHNNY GUITAR, Danish poster

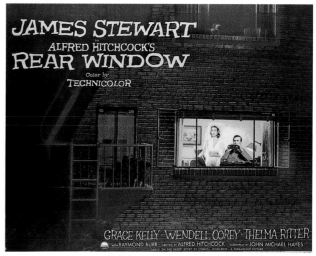

137. REAR WINDOW, half-sheet

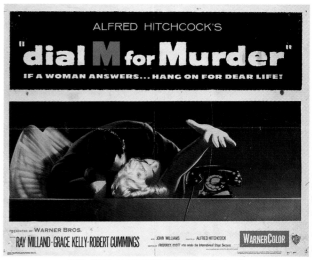

138. DIAL M FOR MURDER, half-sheet

139. SABRINA, half-sheet

140. A STAR IS BORN

Honorable Mentions (other worthy films that also were **NOT** nominated for Best Picture): Brigadoon, Carmen Jones, The Glenn Miller Story, The Wild One
Note: The film that WON the Best Picture Academy Award® is in **BOLD** type. Films that are not presently available for purchase on VHS cassette have an asterisk (*) after their title.

1955: What **WAS** Nominated for the Best Picture Academy Award®:
Marty, Picnic, Mister Roberts, Love is a Many-Splendored Thing, The Rose Tattoo

Here are five worthy films made in 1955 (in no particular order) that the Academy did **NOT** nominate for Best Picture:

141. THE NIGHT OF THE HUNTER*, Lobby Card

143. BAD DAY AT BLACK ROCK, three-sheet

142. THE LADYKILLERS*, British Quad

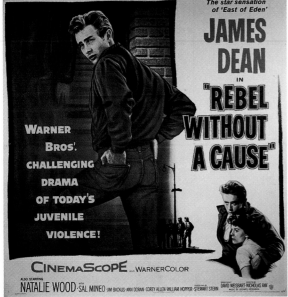

144. REBEL WITHOUT A CAUSE, six-sheet

145. EAST OF EDEN, lobby card

Honorable Mentions (other worthy films that also were **NOT** nominated for Best Picture): The Blackboard Jungle, Oklahoma!, Richard III, Summertime, To Catch a Thief

Note: The film that WON the Best Picture Academy Award® is in **BOLD** type. Films that are not presently available for purchase on VHS cassette have an asterisk (*) after their title.

1956: What **WAS** Nominated for the Best Picture Academy Award®:
Around the World in 80 Days, The King and I, Friendly Persuasion, The Ten Commandments, Giant

Here are five worthy films made in 1956 (in no particular order) that the Academy did **NOT** nominate for Best Picture:

146. THE SEARCHERS, six-sheet

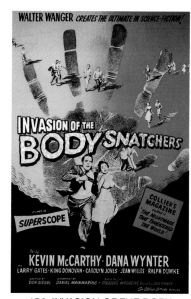

147. BABY DOLL

148. THE COURT JESTER

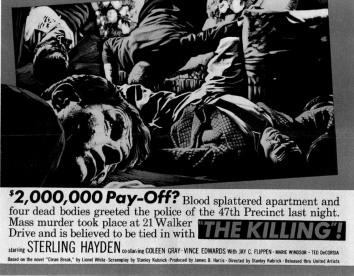

149. THE KILLING, half-sheet

150. INVASION OF THE BODY
SNATCHERS, Forty By Sixty

Honorable Mentions (other worthy films that also were **NOT** nominated for Best Picture):
Attack, Bigger Than Life*, Bus Stop, Forbidden Planet, The Man Who Knew Too Much

Note: The film that WON the Best Picture Academy Award® is in **BOLD** type. Films that are not presently available for purchase on VHS cassette have an asterisk (*) after their title.

1957: What **WAS** Nominated for the Best Picture Academy Award®:
The Bridge on the River Kwai, Peyton Place, 12 Angry Men, Sayonara, Witness for the Prosecution

Here are five worthy films made in 1957 (in no particular order) that the Academy did **NOT** nominate for Best Picture:

151. AN AFFAIR TO REMEMBER

152. A FACE IN THE CROWD

153. PATHS OF GLORY

154. FUNNY FACE,
three-sheet

155. SWEET SMELL OF SUCCESS, lobby card

Honorable Mentions (other worthy films that also were **NOT** nominated for Best Picture):
Gunfight at the O.K. Corral, The Incredible Shrinking Man, Jailhouse Rock, Love in the Afternoon, 3:10 to Yuma

Note: The film that WON the Best Picture Academy Award® is in **BOLD** type. Films that are not presently available for purchase on VHS cassette have an asterisk (*) after their title.

Here are five worthy films made in 1958 (in no particular order) that the Academy did **NOT** nominate for Best Picture:

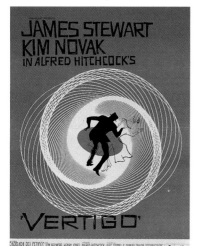

156. VERTIGO, insert

157. A NIGHT TO REMEMBER*, English three-sheet

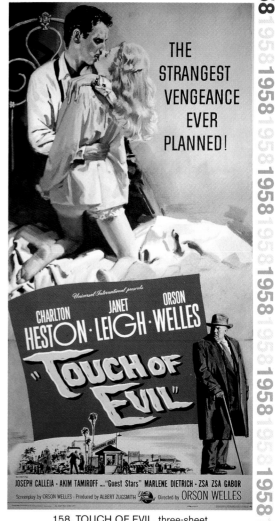

158. TOUCH OF EVIL, three-sheet

159. THE FLY, lobby card

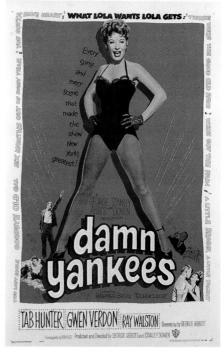

160. DAMN YANKEES

Honorable Mentions (other worthy films that also were **NOT** nominated for Best Picture):
Big Country, I Want to Live!, The Old Man and the Sea, The Seventh Voyage of Sinbad, Some Came Running

Note: The film that WON the Best Picture Academy Award® is in **BOLD** type. Films that are not presently available for purchase on VHS cassette have an asterisk (*) after their title.

1959: What **WAS** Nominated for the Best Picture Academy Award®:

Ben-Hur, Anatomy of a Murder, The Nun's Story, The Diary of Anne Frank, Room at the Top

Here are five worthy films made in 1959 (in no particular order) that the Academy did **NOT** nominate for Best Picture:

161. JOURNEY TO THE CENTER OF THE EARTH, lobby card

162. THE LAST ANGRY MAN, lobby card

163. NORTH BY NORTHWEST, 1963 reissue

164. RIO BRAVO, Argentinian poster

165. SOME LIKE IT HOT, six-sheet

Honorable Mentions (other worthy films that also were **NOT** nominated for Best Picture):

Compulsion, The Mouse that Roared, On the Beach, Pillow Talk, Suddenly, Last Summer

Note: The film that WON the Best Picture Academy Award® is in **BOLD** type. Films that are not presently available for purchase on VHS cassette have an asterisk (*) after their title.

1960: What **WAS** Nominated for the Best Picture Academy Award®:
The Apartment, Elmer Gantry, The Sundowners, Sons and Lovers*, The Alamo

Here are five worthy films made in 1960 (in no particular order) that the Academy did **NOT** nominate for Best Picture:

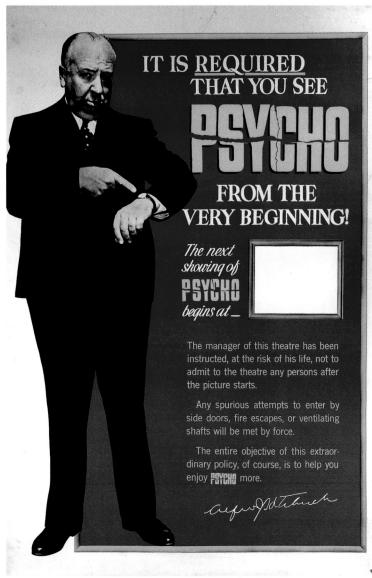

166. PSYCHO, Forty By Sixty

167. SPARTACUS

168. THE TIME MACHINE

169. THE MAGNIFICENT SEVEN, lobby card

170. INHERIT THE WIND

Honorable Mentions (other worthy films that also were **NOT** nominated for Best Picture):
Exodus, Peeping Tom, Saturday Night and Sunday Morning*, Village of the Damned, Wild River*

Note: The film that WON the Best Picture Academy Award® is in **BOLD** type. Films that are not presently available for purchase on VHS cassette have an asterisk (*) after their title.

1961: What **WAS** Nominated for the Best Picture Academy Award®:

West Side Story, Fanny, The Guns of Navarone, The Hustler, Judgment at Nuremberg

Here are five worthy films made in 1961 (in no particular order) that the Academy did **NOT** nominate for Best Picture:

171. BREAKFAST AT TIFFANY'S

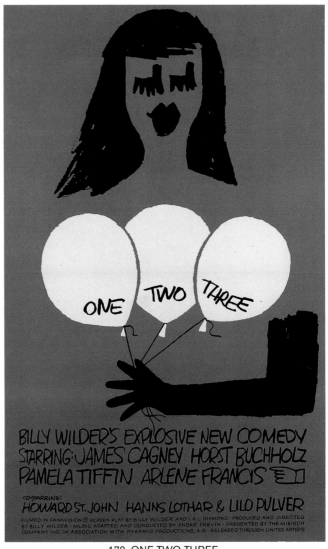

172. ONE TWO THREE

173. THE MISFITS, Spanish poster

174. EL CID

175. SPLENDOR IN THE GRASS,
Japanese poster

Honorable Mentions (other worthy films that also were **NOT** nominated for Best Picture): The Innocents, One Eyed Jacks, The Parent Trap, Shadows, Victim

Note: The film that WON the Best Picture Academy Award® is in **BOLD** type. Films that are not presently available for purchase on VHS cassette have an asterisk (*) after their title.

Here are five worthy films made in 1962 (in no particular order) that the Academy did **NOT** nominate for Best Picture:

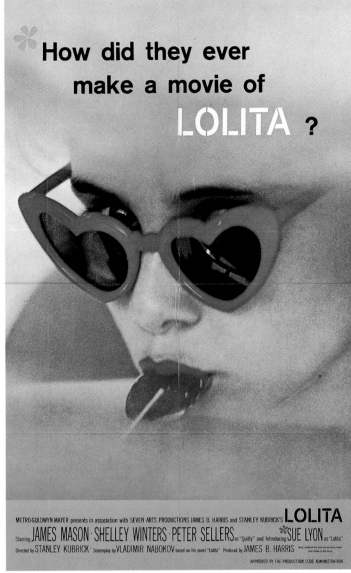

176. LOLITA

177. RIDE THE HIGH COUNTRY

178. BIRDMAN OF ALCATRAZ

179. THE MANCHURIAN CANDIDATE, British Quad

180. THE MAN WHO SHOT
LIBERTY VALANCE

Honorable Mentions (other worthy films that also were **NOT** nominated for Best Picture):
Billy Budd*, Days of Wine and Roses, Long Day's Journey Into Night, The Miracle Worker, Whatever Happened to Baby Jane?

Note: The film that WON the Best Picture Academy Award® is in **BOLD** type. Films that are not presently available for purchase on VHS cassette have an asterisk (*) after their title.

1963: What **WAS** Nominated for the Best Picture Academy Award®:

Tom Jones, Cleopatra, Lilies of the Field, How the West was Won, America America

Here are five worthy films made in 1963 (in no particular order) that the Academy did **NOT** nominate for Best Picture:

181. FROM RUSSIA WITH LOVE, British Quad

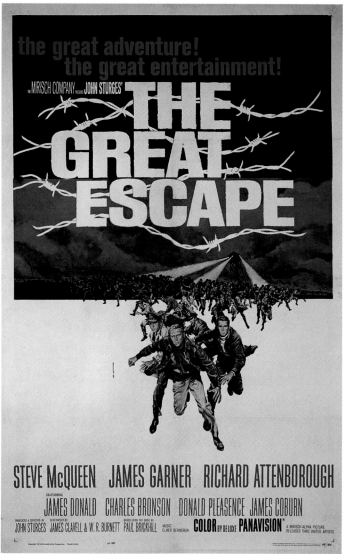

183. THE GREAT ESCAPE

182. THE BIRDS, lobby card

184. HUD

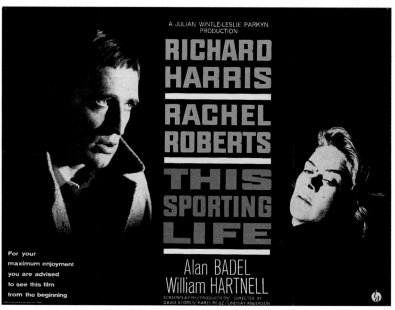

185. THIS SPORTING LIFE*, British Quad

Honorable Mentions (other worthy films that also were **NOT** nominated for Best Picture):

Bye Bye Birdie, Charade, The Haunting, It's a Mad Mad Mad Mad World, The Servant

Note: The film that WON the Best Picture Academy Award® is in **BOLD** type. Films that are not presently available for purchase on VHS cassette have an asterisk (*) after their title.

Here are five worthy films made in 1964 (in no particular order) that the Academy did **NOT** nominate for Best Picture:

186. GOLDFINGER, French poster

187. SEVEN DAYS IN MAY, lobby card

188. A HARD DAY'S NIGHT, lobby card

189. TOPKAPI, lobby card

190. ZULU

Honorable Mentions (other worthy films that also were **NOT** nominated for Best Picture): Fail-Safe, The Night of the Iguana, The Pumpkin Eater, A Shot in the Dark

Note: The film that WON the Best Picture Academy Award® is in **BOLD** type. Films that are not presently available for purchase on VHS cassette have an asterisk (*) after their title.

1965: What **WAS** Nominated for the Best Picture Academy Award®:
The Sound of Music, Darling, Doctor Zhivago, A Thousand Clowns, Ship of Fools

Here are five worthy films made in 1965 (in no particular order) that the Academy did **NOT** nominate for Best Picture:

191. HOW TO MURDER YOUR WIFE

192. THE PAWNBROKER, Japanese poster

193. KING RAT

194. REPULSION, Italian poster

195. CHIMES AT MIDNIGHT, lobby card

Honorable Mentions (other worthy films that also were **NOT** nominated for Best Picture):
Cat Ballou, The Cincinnati Kid, The Flight of the Phoenix, Shenandoah, The Spy Who Came In from the Cold

Note: The film that WON the Best Picture Academy Award® is in **BOLD** type. Films that are not presently available for purchase on VHS cassette have an asterisk (*) after their title.

1966: What **WAS** Nominated for the Best Picture Academy Award®:
A Man for All Seasons, Alfie, The Russians are Coming, The Russians are Coming, The Sand Pebbles, Who's Afraid of Virginia Woolf?

Here are five worthy films made in 1966 (in no particular order) that the Academy did **NOT** nominate for Best Picture:

196. GEORGY GIRL

197. SECONDS

198. A FUNNY THING HAPPENED ON THE WAY TO THE FORUM

199. THE PROFESSIONALS

200. FAHRENHEIT 451

Honorable Mentions (other worthy films that also were **NOT** nominated for Best Picture):
The Fortune Cookie, The Gospel According to St. Matthew, The Naked Prey, The Wrong Box

Note: The film that WON the Best Picture Academy Award® is in **BOLD** type. Films that are not presently available for purchase on VHS cassette have an asterisk (*) after their title.

1967: What **WAS** Nominated for the Best Picture Academy Award®:
In the Heat of the Night, The Graduate, Guess Who's Coming to Dinner, Bonnie and Clyde, Doctor Dolittle

Here are five worthy films made in 1967 (in no particular order) that the Academy did **NOT** nominate for Best Picture:

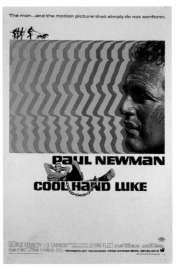

201. COOL HAND LUKE

202. THE DIRTY DOZEN

203. TO SIR, WITH LOVE

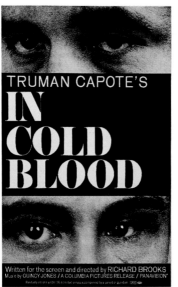

204. IN COLD BLOOD

205. FAR FROM THE MADDING CROWD, lobby card

Honorable Mentions (other worthy films that also were **NOT** nominated for Best Picture): Bedazzled, Don't Look Back, Point Blank, Two for the Road, Wait Until Dark

Note: The film that WON the Best Picture Academy Award® is in **BOLD** type. Films that are not presently available for purchase on VHS cassette have an asterisk (*) after their title.

1968: What **WAS** Nominated for the Best Picture Academy Award®: **Oliver!**, Funny Girl, Romeo and Juliet, Rachel, Rachel*, The Lion in Winter

Here are five worthy films made in 1968 (in no particular order) that the Academy did **NOT** nominate for Best Picture:

206. PLANET OF THE APES

207. TWO THOUSAND AND ONE (2001): A SPACE ODYSSEY

208. THE PRODUCERS

209. ROSEMARY'S BABY

210. THE ODD COUPLE

Honorable Mentions (other worthy films that also were **NOT** nominated for Best Picture):
Bullitt, The Heart Is a Lonely Hunter, If..., Petulia, Pretty Poison*, The Subject was Roses

Note: The film that WON the Best Picture Academy Award® is in **BOLD** type. Films that are not presently available for purchase on VHS cassette have an asterisk (*) after their title.

1969: What **WAS** Nominated for the Best Picture Academy Award®:
Midnight Cowboy, Butch Cassidy and the Sundance Kid, Hello Dolly!, Z, Anne of the Thousand Days

Here are five worthy films made in 1969 (in no particular order) that the Academy did **NOT** nominate for Best Picture:

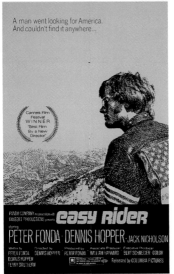

211. EASY RIDER

212. WOMEN IN LOVE

213. THE WILD BUNCH

214. THEY SHOOT HORSES, DON'T THEY?

215. MEDIUM COOL, lobby card

Honorable Mentions (other worthy films that also were **NOT** nominated for Best Picture):
Colossus: The Forbin Project, Once Upon a Time in the West, The Prime of Miss Jean Brodie, Putney Swope*, Take the Money & Run

Note: The film that WON the Best Picture Academy Award® is in **BOLD** type. Films that are not presently available for purchase on VHS cassette have an asterisk (*) after their title.

: What **WAS** Nominated for the Best Picture Academy Award®: **Patton**, Five Easy Pieces, Airport*, M*A*S*H, Love Story
Here are five worthy films made in 1970 (in no particular order) that the Academy did **NOT** nominate for Best Picture:

216. JOE

217. RYAN'S DAUGHTER

218. LITTLE BIG MAN

219. THE PRIVATE LIFE OF SHERLOCK HOLMES, half-sheet

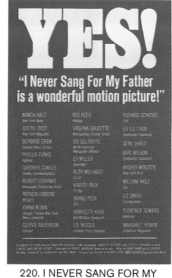

220. I NEVER SANG FOR MY FATHER

Honorable Mentions (other worthy films that also were **NOT** nominated for Best Picture):
The Boys in the Band, Husbands, Lovers and Other Strangers, Where's Poppa?

Note: The film that WON the Best Picture Academy Award® is in **BOLD** type. Films that are not presently available for purchase on VHS cassette have an asterisk (*) after their title.

1971: What **WAS** Nominated for the Best Picture Academy Award®:
The French Connection, A Clockwork Orange, Nicholas and Alexandra, The Last Picture Show, Fiddler on the Roof

Here are five worthy films made in 1971 (in no particular order) that the Academy did **NOT** nominate for Best Picture:

221. THE PANIC IN NEEDLE PARK*

222. THE HOSPITAL

223. DIRTY HARRY, three-sheet

224. MCCABE & MRS. MILLER

225. SUNDAY BLOODY SUNDAY, half-sheet

Honorable Mentions (other worthy films that also were **NOT** nominated for Best Picture):
Carnal Knowledge, Get Carter, Harold and Maude, Klute, Play Misty for Me, Straw Dogs, Walkabout, Willy Wonka & the Chocolate Factory*

Note: The film that WON the Best Picture Academy Award® is in **BOLD** type. Films that are not presently available for purchase on VHS cassette have an asterisk (*) after their title.

1972: What **WAS** Nominated for the Best Picture Academy Award®: **The Godfather**, Deliverance, Cabaret, The Emigrants, Sounder

Here are five worthy films made in 1972 (in no particular order) that the Academy did **NOT** nominate for Best Picture:

226. PLAY IT AGAIN, SAM

227. SLEUTH

228. WHAT'S UP, DOC?

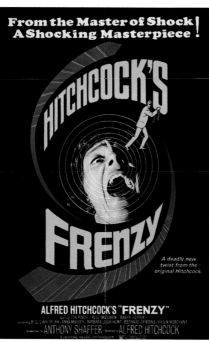

229. FRENZY

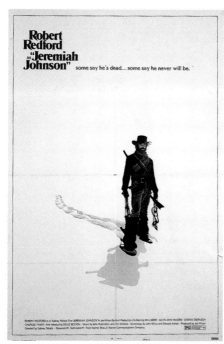

230. JEREMIAH JOHNSON

Honorable Mentions (other worthy films that also were **NOT** nominated for Best Picture):
The Getaway, The Candidate, The Hot Rock*, Images*, The Ruling Class, Last Tango in Paris, Slaughterhouse-Five

Note: The film that WON the Best Picture Academy Award® is in **BOLD** type. Films that are not presently available for purchase on VHS cassette have an asterisk (*) after their title.

1973: What **WAS** Nominated for the Best Picture Academy Award®:
The Sting, American Graffiti, Cries and Whispers, A Touch of Class*, The Exorcist

Here are five worthy films made in 1973 (in no particular order) that the Academy did **NOT** nominate for Best Picture:

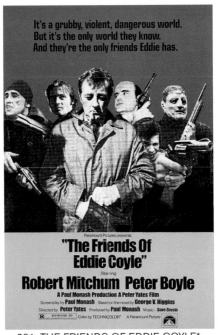

231. THE FRIENDS OF EDDIE COYLE*

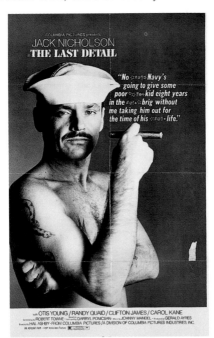

232. THE LAST DETAIL

233. SERPICO

234. THE WICKER MAN, English one-sheet

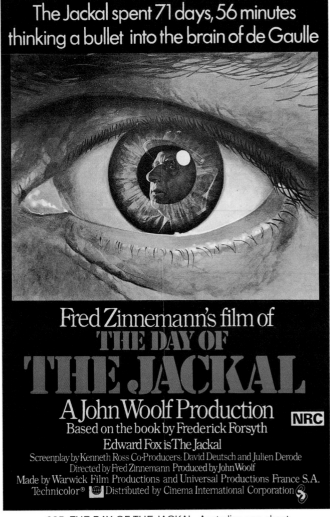

235. THE DAY OF THE JACKAL, Australian one-sheet

Honorable Mentions (other worthy films that also were **NOT** nominated for Best Picture):
Badlands, Charley Varrick, Don't Look Now, Mean Streets, Paper Moon, Papillon

Note: The film that WON the Best Picture Academy Award® is in **BOLD** type. Films that are not presently available for purchase on VHS cassette have an asterisk (*) after their title.

1974: What **WAS** Nominated for the Best Picture Academy Award®:
The Godfather Part II, The Conversation, The Towering Inferno, Chinatown, Lenny

Here are five worthy films made in 1974 (in no particular order) that the Academy did **NOT** nominate for Best Picture:

236. THE PARALLAX VIEW

237. THE TAKING OF PELHAM ONE TWO THREE

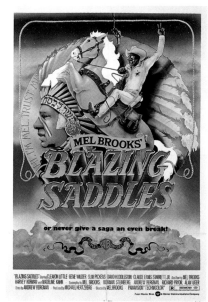

238. BLAZING SADDLES

239. ALICE DOESN'T LIVE HERE ANYMORE

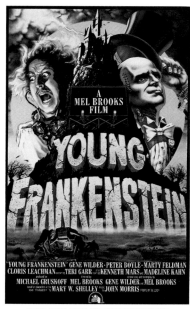

240. YOUNG FRANKENSTEIN

Honorable Mentions (other worthy films that also were **NOT** nominated for Best Picture): California Split, Harry and Tonto, The Sugarland Express, Thieves Like Us

Note: The film that WON the Best Picture Academy Award® is in **BOLD** type. Films that are not presently available for purchase on VHS cassette have an asterisk (*) after their title.

1975: What **WAS** Nominated for the Best Picture Academy Award®:

One Flew Over the Cuckoo's Nest, Barry Lyndon, Dog Day Afternoon, Nashville, Jaws

Here are five worthy films made in 1975 (in no particular order) that the Academy did ***NOT*** nominate for Best Picture:

241. THE MAN WHO WOULD BE KING

242. MONTY PYTHON AND THE HOLY GRAIL

243. SHAMPOO

244. SMILE

245. NIGHT MOVES*, British Quad

Honorable Mentions (other worthy films that also were ***NOT*** nominated for Best Picture):

Love and Death, Picnic at Hanging Rock, The Sunshine Boys, Three Days of the Condor

Note: The film that WON the Best Picture Academy Award® is in ***BOLD*** type. Films that are not presently available for purchase on VHS cassette have an asterisk (*) after their title.

Here are five worthy films made in 1976 (in no particular order) that the Academy did **NOT** nominate for Best Picture:

246. ROBIN AND MARIAN

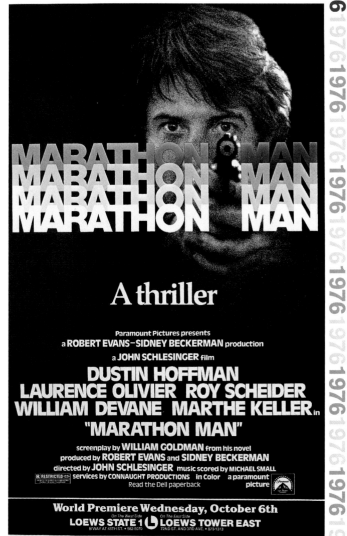

247. MARATHON MAN

248. THE SHOOTIST

249. THE BAD NEWS BEARS

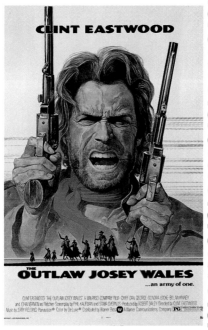

250. THE OUTLAW JOSEY WALES

Honorable Mentions (other worthy films that also were **NOT** nominated for Best Picture): Carrie, The Front, The Man Who Fell to Earth, The Omen

Note: The film that WON the Best Picture Academy Award® is in **BOLD** type. Films that are not presently available for purchase on VHS cassette have an asterisk (*) after their title.

1977: What **WAS** Nominated for the Best Picture Academy Award®: **Annie Hall**, Star Wars, The Turning Point, Julia, The Goodbye Girl

Here are five worthy films made in 1977 (in no particular order) that the Academy did **NOT** nominate for Best Picture:

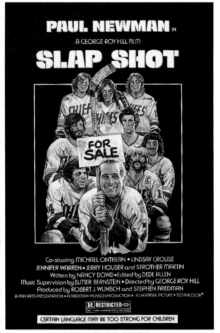

251. SLAP SHOT

252. CLOSE ENCOUNTERS OF THE THIRD KIND

253. THE LAST WAVE*

254. SATURDAY NIGHT FEVER

255. LOOKING FOR MR. GOODBAR

Honorable Mentions (other worthy films that also were **NOT** nominated for Best Picture): The Duellists, Eraserhead*, Kentucky Fried Movie, Three Women*

Note: The film that WON the Best Picture Academy Award® is in **BOLD** type. Films that are not presently available for purchase on VHS cassette have an asterisk (*) after their title.

1978: What **WAS** Nominated for the Best Picture Academy Award®:
The Deer Hunter, Heaven Can Wait, Midnight Express, An Unmarried Woman, Coming Home

Here are five worthy films made in 1978 (in no particular order) that the Academy did **NOT** nominate for Best Picture:

256. DAYS OF HEAVEN

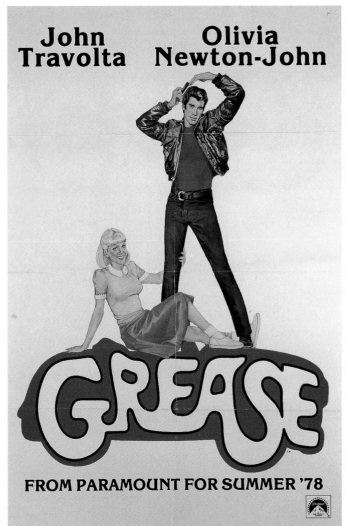

257. GREASE

258. INTERIORS

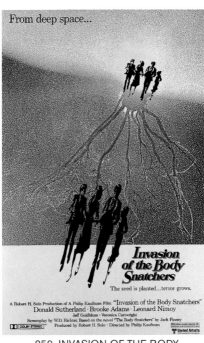

259. INVASION OF THE BODY SNATCHERS

260. NATIONAL LAMPOON'S ANIMAL HOUSE, 1982 reissue

Honorable Mentions (other worthy films that also were **NOT** nominated for Best Picture): American Hot Wax*, Fingers, Go Tell the Spartans, Pretty Baby, Superman

Note: The film that WON the Best Picture Academy Award® is in **BOLD** type. Films that are not presently available for purchase on VHS cassette have an asterisk (*) after their title.

1979: What **WAS** Nominated for the Best Picture Academy Award®:

Kramer vs. Kramer, Apocalypse Now, Norma Rae, All That Jazz*, Breaking Away

Here are five worthy films made in 1979 (in no particular order) that the Academy did **NOT** nominate for Best Picture:

261. THE GREAT SANTINI

262. THE IN-LAWS

263. THE WANDERERS

264. BEING THERE

265. MANHATTAN, British Quad

Honorable Mentions (other worthy films that also were **NOT** nominated for Best Picture):

The Black Stallion, The China Syndrome, Hair, Monty Python's Life of Brian, My Brilliant Career*, The Onion Field*, Ten

Note: The film that WON the Best Picture Academy Award® is in **BOLD** type. Films that are not presently available for purchase on VHS cassette have an asterisk (*) after their title.

1980: What **WAS** Nominated for the Best Picture Academy Award®:
Ordinary People, Raging Bull, The Elephant Man, Coal Miner's Daughter, Tess

Here are five worthy films made in 1980 (in no particular order) that the Academy did **NOT** nominate for Best Picture:

266. STARDUST MEMORIES

267. AIRPLANE!

268. MELVIN AND HOWARD

269. THE SHINING, British Quad

270. THE STUNT MAN

Honorable Mentions (other worthy films that also were **NOT** nominated for Best Picture): Breaker Morant, The Long Good Friday*, Resurrection, Used Cars

Note: The film that WON the Best Picture Academy Award® is in **BOLD** type. Films that are not presently available for purchase on VHS cassette have an asterisk (*) after their title.

1981: What **WAS** Nominated for the Best Picture Academy Award®: **Chariots of Fire**, Atlantic City, Raiders of the Lost Ark, Reds, On Golden Pond
Here are five worthy films made in 1981 (in no particular order) that the Academy did **NOT** nominate for Best Picture:

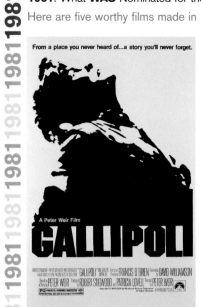

271. GALLIPOLI

272. GREGORY'S GIRL*, British Quad

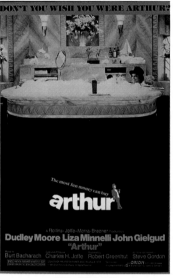

273. ARTHUR

274. PENNIES FROM HEAVEN

275. MODERN ROMANCE

Honorable Mentions (other worthy films that also were **NOT** nominated for Best Picture): Body Heat, Cutter's Way, Excalibur, Prince of the City, Ragtime
Note: The film that WON the Best Picture Academy Award® is in **BOLD** type. Films that are not presently available for purchase on VHS cassette have an asterisk (*) after their title.

1982: What **WAS** Nominated for the Best Picture Academy Award®: **Gandhi**, Tootsie, The Verdict, Missing, E.T. the Extra-Terrestrial

Here are five worthy films made in 1982 (in no particular order) that the Academy did **NOT** nominate for Best Picture:

276. FAST TIMES AT RIDGEMONT HIGH

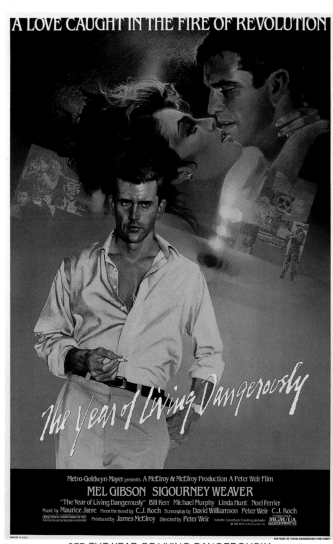

277. THE YEAR OF LIVING DANGEROUSLY

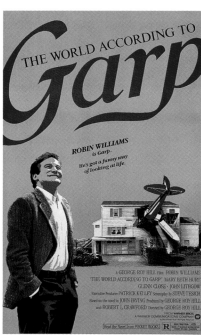

278. THE WORLD ACCORDING TO GARP

279. DINER

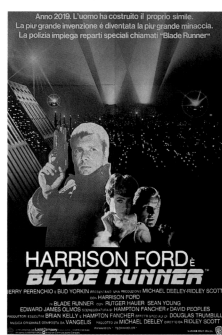

280. BLADE RUNNER, German poster

Honorable Mentions (other worthy films that also were **NOT** nominated for Best Picture):
The Grey Fox*, My Favorite Year, An Officer and a Gentleman, Shoot the Moon, Sophie's Choice, Victor/Victoria

Note: The film that WON the Best Picture Academy Award® is in **BOLD** type. Films that are not presently available for purchase on VHS cassette have an asterisk (*) after their title.

1983: What **WAS** Nominated for the Best Picture Academy Award®:
Terms of Endearment, The Big Chill, The Dresser, Tender Mercies*, The Right Stuff

Here are five worthy films made in 1983 (in no particular order) that the Academy did **NOT** nominate for Best Picture:

281. SILKWOOD

282. THE KING OF COMEDY

283. UNDER FIRE

284. LOCAL HERO

285. A CHRISTMAS STORY, German poster

Honorable Mentions (other worthy films that also were **NOT** nominated for Best Picture):
Baby, It's You, Heart Like a Wheel, Monty Python's The Meaning of Life, Never Cry Wolf, Risky Business

Note: The film that WON the Best Picture Academy Award® is in **BOLD** type. Films that are not presently available for purchase on VHS cassette have an asterisk (*) after their title.

1984: What **WAS** Nominated for the Best Picture Academy Award®:
Amadeus, A Passage to India, A Soldier's Story, Places in the Heart, The Killing Fields

Here are five worthy films made in 1984 (in no particular order) that the Academy did **NOT** nominate for Best Picture:

286. THE NATURAL

287. THE TERMINATOR

288. BLOOD SIMPLE

289. ONCE UPON A TIME IN AMERICA

290. BROADWAY DANNY ROSE*

Honorable Mentions (other worthy films that also were **NOT** nominated for Best Picture):
Indiana Jones and the Temple of Doom, The Karate Kid, Stranger Than Paradise, This Is Spinal Tap

Note: The film that WON the Best Picture Academy Award® is in **BOLD** type. Films that are not presently available for purchase on VHS cassette have an asterisk (*) after their title.

1985: What **WAS** Nominated for the Best Picture Academy Award®:
Out of Africa, The Color Purple, Kiss of the Spider Woman*, Prizzi's Honor, Witness

Here are five worthy films made in 1985 (in no particular order) that the Academy did **NOT** nominate for Best Picture:

291. BACK TO THE FUTURE*

292. AFTER HOURS

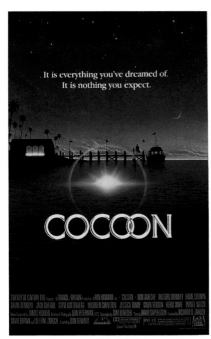

293. COCOON

294. RUNAWAY TRAIN

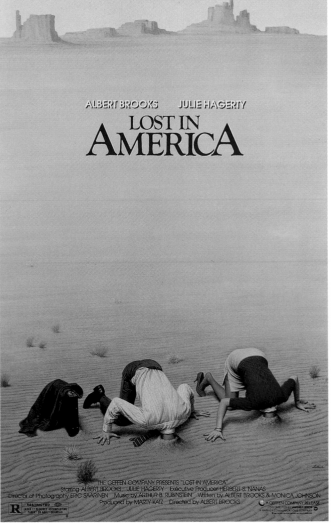

295. LOST IN AMERICA

Honorable Mentions (other worthy films that also were **NOT** nominated for Best Picture): Brazil, The Purple Rose of Cairo, Silverado, The Trip to Bountiful*

Note: The film that WON the Best Picture Academy Award® is in **BOLD** type. Films that are not presently available for purchase on VHS cassette have an asterisk (*) after their title.

1986: What **WAS** Nominated for the Best Picture Academy Award®:
Platoon, Hannah and Her Sisters*, Children of a Lesser God, A Room with a View, The Mission

Here are five worthy films made in 1986 (in no particular order) that the Academy did **NOT** nominate for Best Picture:

296. HOOSIERS

297. BLUE VELVET

298. 'ROUND MIDNIGHT

299. MONA LISA*, British Quad

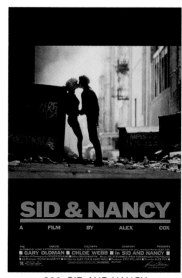

300. SID AND NANCY

Honorable Mentions (other worthy films that also were **NOT** nominated for Best Picture): Ferris Bueller's Day Off, Little Shop of Horrors, Manhunter, Something Wild

Note: The film that WON the Best Picture Academy Award® is in **BOLD** type. Films that are not presently available for purchase on VHS cassette have an asterisk (*) after their title.

1987: What **WAS** Nominated for the Best Picture Academy Award®:
The Last Emperor, Hope and Glory, Broadcast News, Fatal Attraction, Moonstruck

Here are five worthy films made in 1987 (in no particular order) that the Academy did **NOT** nominate for Best Picture:

301. HOUSE OF GAMES

304. THE PRINCESS BRIDE, British Quad

302. FULL METAL JACKET

303. RAISING ARIZONA

305. PLANES, TRAINS & AUTOMOBILES

Honorable Mentions (other worthy films that also were **NOT** nominated for Best Picture):
The Big Easy, Empire of the Sun, Good Morning, Vietnam, RoboCop, Stand and Deliver, The Stepfather*

Note: The film that WON the Best Picture Academy Award® is in **BOLD** type. Films that are not presently available for purchase on VHS cassette have an asterisk (*) after their title.

1988: What **WAS** Nominated for the Best Picture Academy Award®:
Rain Man, Dangerous Liaisons, Working Girl, The Accidental Tourist, Mississippi Burning

Here are five worthy films made in 1988 (in no particular order) that the Academy did **NOT** nominate for Best Picture:

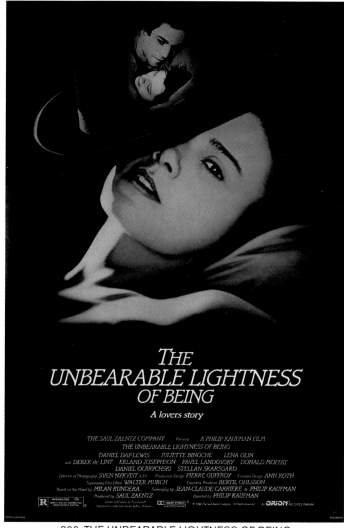

306. THE UNBEARABLE LIGHTNESS OF BEING

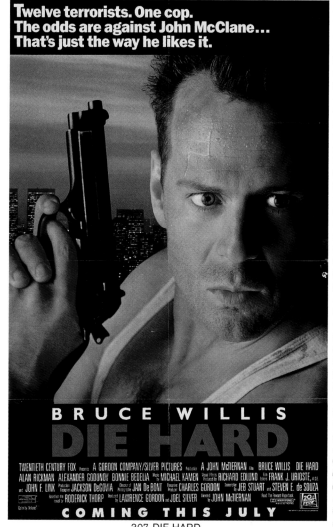

307. DIE HARD

308. BIG

309. WHO FRAMED ROGER RABBIT?

310. BULL DURHAM

Honorable Mentions (other worthy films that also were **NOT** nominated for Best Picture):
The Accused, Beetlejuice, Dead Ringers*, A Fish Called Wanda, The Last Temptation of Christ

Note: The film that WON the Best Picture Academy Award® is in **BOLD** type. Films that are not presently available for purchase on VHS cassette have an asterisk (*) after their title.

1989: What **WAS** Nominated for the Best Picture Academy Award®:
Driving Miss Daisy, My Left Foot, Dead Poets Society, Born on the Fourth of July, Field of Dreams

Here are five worthy films made in 1989 (in no particular order) that the Academy did **NOT** nominate for Best Picture:

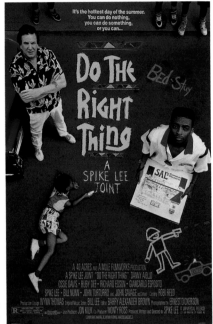

311. DO THE RIGHT THING

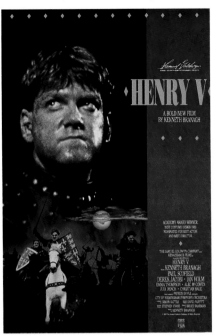

312. HENRY V

313. SEX, LIES, AND VIDEOTAPE

314. SAY ANYTHING...

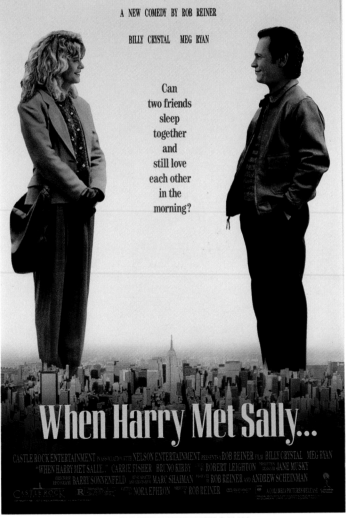

315. WHEN HARRY MET SALLY

Honorable Mentions (other worthy films that also were **NOT** nominated for Best Picture):
Crimes and Misdemeanors*, Drugstore Cowboy, The Fabulous Baker Boys, Glory, Heathers, Mystery Train, Parenthood
Note: The film that WON the Best Picture Academy Award® is in **BOLD** type. Films that are not presently available for purchase on VHS cassette have an asterisk (*) after their title.

1990: What **WAS** Nominated for the Best Picture Academy Award®:
Dances with Wolves, Goodfellas, The Godfather Part III, Ghost, Awakenings

Here are five worthy films made in 1990 (in no particular order) that the Academy did **NOT** nominate for Best Picture:

316. LONGTIME COMPANION

317. EDWARD SCISSORHANDS

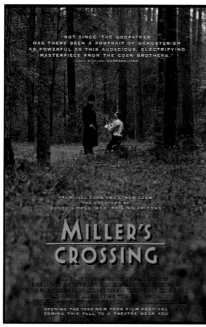

318. MILLER'S CROSSING

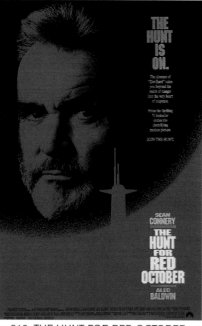

319. THE HUNT FOR RED OCTOBER

320. THE GRIFTERS

Honorable Mentions (other worthy films that also were **NOT** nominated for Best Picture): Avalon, Pretty Woman, Reversal of Fortune

Note: The film that WON the Best Picture Academy Award® is in **BOLD** type. Films that are not presently available for purchase on VHS cassette have an asterisk (*) after their title.

1991: What **WAS** Nominated for the Best Picture Academy Award®:
The Silence of the Lambs, Beauty and the Beast*, JFK, Busgy, The Prince of Tides

Here are five worthy films made in 1991 (in no particular order) that the Academy did **NOT** nominate for Best Picture:

321. HEAR MY SONG

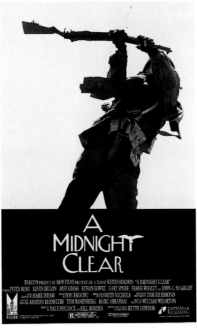

322. A MIDNIGHT CLEAR

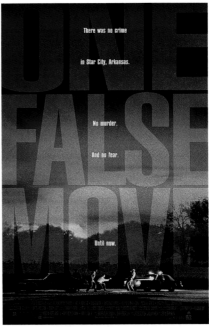

323. ONE FALSE MOVE

324. FRIED GREEN TOMATOES

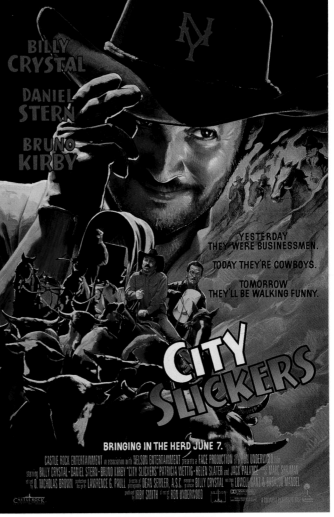

325. CITY SLICKERS

Honorable Mentions (other worthy films that also were **NOT** nominated for Best Picture):
Barton Fink, Boyz N the Hood, The Commitments, For the Boys, The Rapture, Soapdish

Note: The film that WON the Best Picture Academy Award® is in **BOLD** type. Films that are not presently available for purchase on VHS cassette have an asterisk (*) after their title.

1992: What **WAS** Nominated for the Best Picture Academy Award®:
Unforgiven, The Crying Game, A Few Good Men, Howards End, Scent of a Woman

Here are five worthy films made in 1992 (in no particular order) that the Academy did **NOT** nominate for Best Picture:

326. MY COUSIN VINNY

327. RESERVOIR DOGS

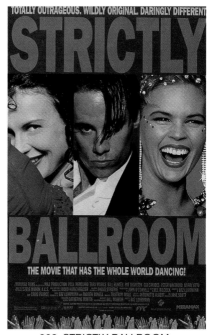

328. STRICTLY BALLROOM

329. THE LAST OF THE MOHICANS

330. THE PLAYER

Honorable Mentions (other worthy films that also were **NOT** nominated for Best Picture):
Aladdin*, Basic Instinct, Glengarry Glen Ross, Honeymoon in Vegas, A League of Their Own

Note: The film that WON the Best Picture Academy Award® is in **BOLD** type. Films that are not presently available for purchase on VHS cassette have an asterisk (*) after their title.

1993: What **WAS** Nominated for the Best Picture Academy Award®:

Schindler's List, The Remains of the Day, The Fugitive, In the Name of the Father, The Piano

Here are five worthy films made in 1993 (in no particular order) that the Academy did **NOT** nominate for Best Picture:

331. RUDY

332. SLEEPLESS IN SEATTLE

333. IN THE LINE OF FIRE

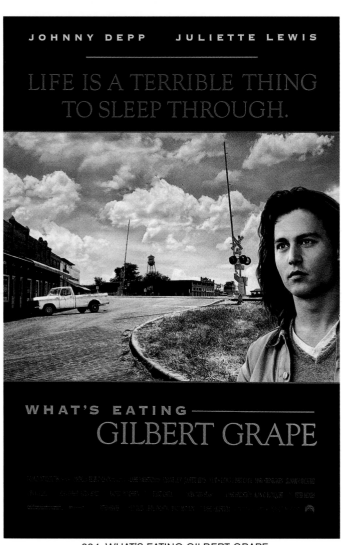

334. WHAT'S EATING GILBERT GRAPE

335. GROUNDHOG DAY

Honorable Mentions (other worthy films that also were **NOT** nominated for Best Picture):

Dave, The Joy Luck Club, Mrs. Doubtfire, Philadelphia, Six Degrees of Separation

Note: The film that WON the Best Picture Academy Award® is in **BOLD** type. Films that are not presently available for purchase on VHS cassette have an asterisk (*) after their title.

1994: What **WAS** Nominated for the Best Picture Academy Award®:
Forrest Gump, Pulp Fiction, Four Weddings and a Funeral, The Shawshank Redemption, Quiz Show
Here are five worthy films made in 1994 (in no particular order) that the Academy did **NOT** nominate for Best Picture:

336. CLERKS

337. THE LION KING*

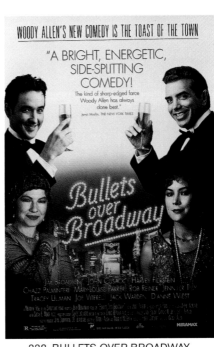

338. BULLETS OVER BROADWAY

339. ED WOOD

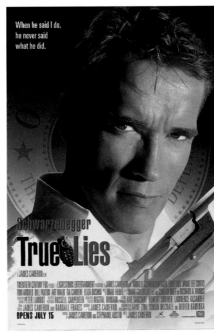

340. TRUE LIES

Honorable Mentions (other worthy films that also were **NOT** nominated for Best Picture): Interview With the Vampire, Muriel's Wedding, Once Were Warriors, Speed

Note: The film that WON the Best Picture Academy Award® is in **BOLD** type. Films that are not presently available for purchase on VHS cassette have an asterisk (*) after their title.

1995: What **WAS** Nominated for the Best Picture Academy Award®: **Braveheart**, Babe, Apollo 13, The Postman, Sense and Sensibility

Here are five worthy films made in 1995 (in no particular order) that the Academy did **NOT** nominate for Best Picture:

341. ROB ROY

342. CLUELESS

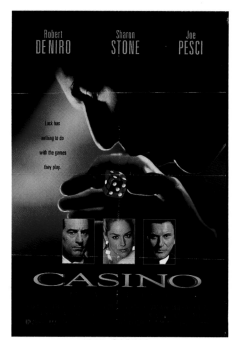

343. CASINO

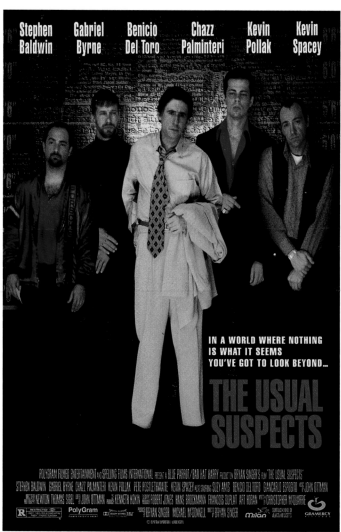

344. THE USUAL SUSPECTS

345. TOY STORY

Honorable Mentions (other worthy films that also were **NOT** nominated for Best Picture):

Ace Ventura: When Nature Calls, The American President, The Bridges of Madison County, Dead Man, Leaving Las Vegas

Note: The film that WON the Best Picture Academy Award® is in **BOLD** type. Films that are not presently available for purchase on VHS cassette have an asterisk (*) after their title.

1996: What **WAS** Nominated for the Best Picture Academy Award®: **The English Patient**, Shine, Secrets & Lies, Jerry Maguire, Fargo
Here are five worthy films made in 1996 (in no particular order) that the Academy did **NOT** nominate for Best Picture:

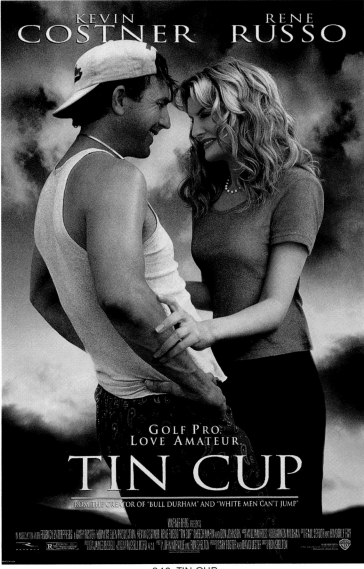

346. TIN CUP

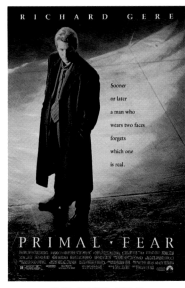

348. PRIMAL FEAR

349. LONE STAR

347. SLING BLADE, British Quad

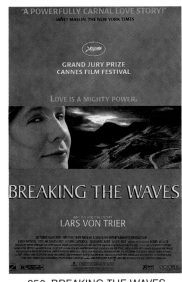

350. BREAKING THE WAVES

Honorable Mentions (other worthy films that also were **NOT** nominated for Best Picture): Independence Day, Mars Attacks!, The People vs. Larry Flynt, Trainspotting

Note: The film that WON the Best Picture Academy Award® is in **BOLD** type. Films that are not presently available for purchase on VHS cassette have an asterisk (*) after their title.

1997: What **WAS** Nominated for the Best Picture Academy Award®:
Titanic, L.A. Confidential, Good Will Hunting, As Good as it Gets, The Full Monty

Here are five worthy films made in 1997 (in no particular order) that the Academy did **NOT** nominate for Best Picture:

351. THE SPANISH PRISONER, British Quad

352. AMISTAD

353. DONNIE BRASCO

354. WAG THE DOG

355. THE SWEET HEREAFTER

Honorable Mentions (other worthy films that also were **NOT** nominated for Best Picture): In & Out, In the Company of Men, Men in Black, My Best Friend's Wedding

Note: The film that WON the Best Picture Academy Award® is in **BOLD** type. Films that are not presently available for purchase on VHS cassette have an asterisk (*) after their title.

1998: What **WAS** Nominated for the Best Picture Academy Award®:
Shakespeare in Love, Elizabeth, Life is Beautiful, Saving Private Ryan, The Thin Red Line,
Here are five worthy films made in 1998 (in no particular order) that the Academy did **NOT** nominate for Best Picture:

356. THE TRUMAN SHOW

357. THERE'S SOMETHING ABOUT MARY

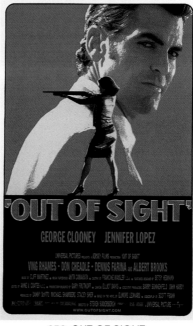

358. OUT OF SIGHT

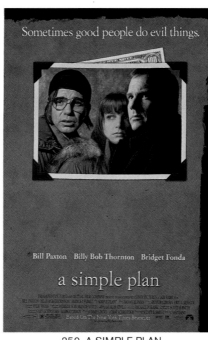

359. A SIMPLE PLAN

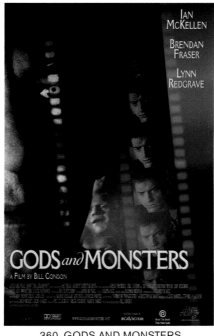

360. GODS AND MONSTERS

Honorable Mentions (other worthy films that also were **NOT** nominated for Best Picture): Beloved, A Bug's Life, Bulworth, Smoke Signals

Note: The film that WON the Best Picture Academy Award® is in **BOLD** type. Films that are not presently available for purchase on VHS cassette have an asterisk (*) after their title.

1999: What **WAS** Nominated for the Best Picture Academy Award®:

American Beauty, The Cider House Rules, The Green Mile, The Insider, The Sixth Sense

Here are five worthy films made in 1999 (in no particular order) that the Academy did ***NOT*** nominate for Best Picture:

361. TOY STORY 2

BEING JOHN MALKOVICH

362. BEING JOHN MALKOVICH

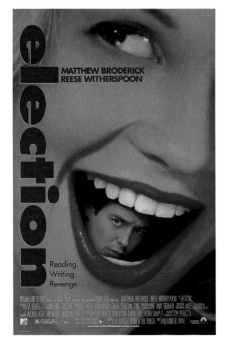

363. ELECTION

364. BOYS DON'T CRY

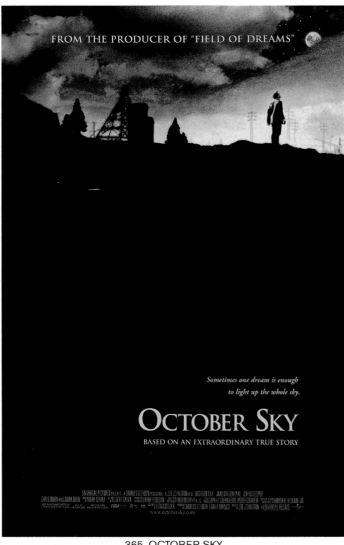

365. OCTOBER SKY

Honorable Mentions (other worthy films that also were **NOT** nominated for Best Picture): Eyes Wide Shut, Fight Club, The Iron Giant, Magnolia

Note: The film that WON the Best Picture Academy Award® is in ***BOLD*** type. Films that are not presently available for purchase on VHS cassette have an asterisk (*) after their title.

2000: What **WAS** Nominated for the Best Picture Academy Award®:
Gladiator, Chocolat*, Crouching Tiger, Hidden Dragon*, Erin Brockovich, Traffic*

Here are five worthy films made in 2000 (in no particular order) that the Academy did **NOT** nominate for Best Picture:

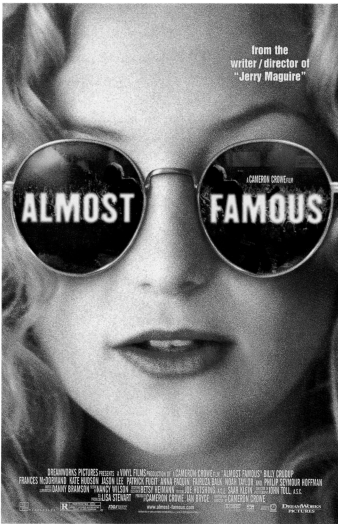

366. ALMOST FAMOUS

367. CAST AWAY

368. HIGH FIDELITY

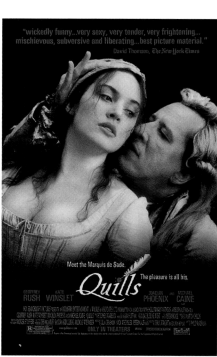

369. QUILLS

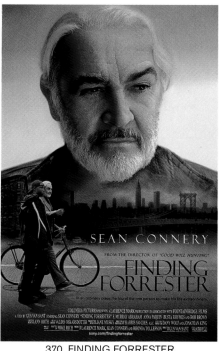

370. FINDING FORRESTER

Honorable Mentions (other worthy films that also were **NOT** nominated for Best Picture):The Contender, Billy Elliot, Wonder Boys, You Can Count On Me*

Note: The film that WON the Best Picture Academy Award® is in **BOLD** type. Films that are not presently available for purchase on VHS cassette have an asterisk (*) after their title.

NOT *Nominated*
MOVIE POSTERS INDEX

Films that are not presently available for purchase on VHS cassette have an asterisk (*) after their title.

NOT Nominated
MOVIE POSTERS INDEX

Films that are not presently available for purchase on VHS cassette have an asterisk (*) after their title.

NOT Nominated
MOVIE POSTERS INDEX

Films that are not presently available for purchase on VHS cassette have an asterisk (*) after their title.